The Library of Physics™

FORCES IN NATURE

Understanding Gravitational, Electrical, and Magnetic Force

Liz Sonneborn

The Rosen Publishing Group, Inc., New York

Published in 2005 by The Rosen Publishing Group, Inc.
29 East 21st Street, New York, NY 10010

Library of Congress Cataloging-in-Publication Data

Sonneborn, Liz.
Forces in nature: understanding gravitational, electrical, and magnetic force / Liz Sonneborn.
   p. cm.— (The library of physics)
Includes bibliographical references and index.
ISBN 1-4042-0332-X (library binding)
1. Electromagnetism. 2. Gravitation.
I. Title. II. Series: Library of physics (Rosen Publishing Group)
QC760.S67 2004
537'.54—dc22

2004011072

On the cover: An image of Jupiter and its moons, illustrating the gravitational force at work on celestial bodies in orbit

Manufactured in the United States of America

Contents

Imagine coming home from school one afternoon. You first toss your backpack on the kitchen table and then turn on the television. You notice the room is too dark, so you open the curtains to let in some light.

It may not seem like you have done anything special. But in a few simple actions, you have come in contact with the four fundamental forces in nature.

When your backpack landed on the table, you saw evidence of the gravitational force. Earth's gravitational pull made the backpack fall down toward the table. If the gravitational force were not acting on it, it would have floated in the air.

When the television came on, you came in contact with the electromagnetic force. This force accounts for the electricity that powers your television set. It is also responsible for the television waves that produce the images you watch.

When you opened the curtains, you came in contact with the weak force. This force most often governs radioactive decay, but it also allows the Sun to burn.

And when you walked into your home, everything around you was evidence of the strong force. The strong force binds together the nuclei of atoms that make up everything in our world.

Few people besides physicists ever think about the fundamental forces around them. But everywhere and all the time, their effect helps shape the world we live in.

1

The Gravitational Force

A child drops a ball. The ball falls to Earth. This simple act is evidence of the invisible force that attracts each object in the universe to every other object—the gravitational force. Much less simple are the laws ruling gravitation. In many ways, gravitation remains for scientists the most mysterious of the four fundamental forces in nature.

Newton's Law

Observing the effects of gravitation, ancient philosophers believed the earth was the natural resting place of all things. Greek philosopher Aristotle developed a slightly more sophisticated theory, maintaining that objects were pulled to the earth at a speed proportional to their size. A millennium later, legend has it, the Italian astronomer Galileo tested this idea by dropping objects of various size from the Tower of Pisa. Galileo concluded that, if the effect of air resistance is eliminated, all objects fall the same speed regardless of size.

In the late seventeenth century, our understanding of gravitation grew enormously through the work of British philosopher and mathematician Sir Isaac Newton. Newton was studying why the planets in the solar system orbited around the Sun in well-defined paths. He concluded that an attractive force was acting on the Sun and each planet. More important, he devised a mathematical expression of this force with his law of universal gravitation.

It was through a rivalry with fellow physicist Robert Hooke that Sir Isaac Newton *(above)* developed his law of universal gravitation. The ideas that Hooke shared in their correspondence inspired Newton to apply his theories regarding attraction to the planets.

According to Newton's law, the gravitational force (*F*) between two bodies (m_1 and m_2) can be calculated using the following equation:

$$F = \frac{Gm_1m_2}{r^2}$$

where *r* is the distance between the two bodies and *G* is a constant. (Later experiments calculated the value of this universal constant of gravitation as 6.670×10^{-11} newton-meters^2/kilograms^2.)

Newton's law explains that the size of a gravitational force between two objects is proportional to the product of their masses. Imagine two objects placed at a set distance from each other. One has a mass of two kilograms, and the other has a mass of four kilograms, so the product of their masses is eight. Let's assume the gravitational force between them is equal to 1 newton. (A newton is a unit of measuring force.)

Now imagine doubling the size of these two masses, without changing the distance between them. One object now has a mass of four kilograms, and the other has a mass of eight kilograms, so the product of their two masses is thirty-two. In the second example, this product is four times larger than that in the first example. By Newton's law, the force between them will be four times larger as well, so the force in the second example has to be equal to four newtons.

Newton's law also indicates that the gravitational force between two objects decreases as the distance between them increases and vice versa. More precisely, the size of the force is the inverse square of the distance between them ($1/r^2$).

This time, imagine two objects set at one meter apart with a gravitational force of one newton between them. If the distance between them is

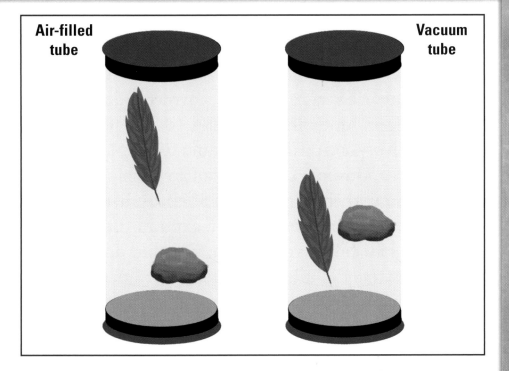

This diagram illustrates Galileo's findings regarding gravitational force. The tube on the left is filled with air. Note that because the feather is so light, it is slowed down by the air. Since the stone is much heavier than air, it falls at a faster rate. Though they are different weights, the two objects fall at the same speed in the tube on the right, which is devoid of air.

doubled to two meters, the force will decrease to 1/4 newton ($r = 2$, so the force equals $1/2^2$, or 1/4).

What happens if we half the distance between the two objects? The force will increase to 4 newtons; $r = 1/2$, so the force equals $1/(1/2)^2$, or $1/(1/4)$, or 4.

Testing Newton

In the nineteenth century, some astronomical calculations called Newton's law into question. Astronomers found that the orbit of the planet Uranus follows a path different from the one that was charted using Newton's equations. But soon this seeming contradiction of Newton's theories provided more evidence that the theories were actually correct.

Working independently in the 1840s, two astronomers—John Couch Adams of England and Urbain-Jean-Joseph Leverrier of France—used Newton's law to chart the orbit of an undiscovered planet. Its pull on Uranus could explain the planet's peculiar path. A few years later, German astronomer Johann Gottfried Galle confirmed their speculation by discovering Neptune traveling in the precise path

Dark Matter

From the motion of stars, astronomers have concluded that much of the universe is made up of dark matter. Like ordinary matter, dark matter is affected by the gravitational force. But, because it does not form stars that emit light, it is invisible, hence its name. Though, through the laws of gravitation, astronomers know dark matter exists, they have yet to determine exactly what constitutes it.

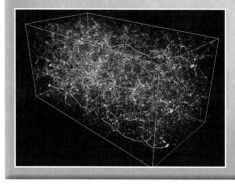

This is a computer model of a dark matter map. The dark matter is shown in red.

Leverrier had laid out. In the twentieth century, Pluto was discovered in much the same way.

Newton's law of universal gravitation remained unchallenged for hundreds of years. It still ably defines the force of attraction between most objects in the physical world. But since 1915, when Albert Einstein formulated the general theory of relativity, physicists have realized that under certain conditions the Newtonian law of gravitation no longer holds true. For instance, Einstein's theory is needed to explain the extremely strong gravitational pull between massive objects with little distance separating them.

Changes in Gravitation

A planet's gravitational pull on objects on its surface is called weight. Weight should not be confused with mass. Mass—the amount of matter in an object—is constant. The mass of an object remains the same, regardless of whether the object sits on Earth, on the Moon, or on Jupiter.

But an object's weight can change. It weighs more on Jupiter than on Earth. Since Jupiter is far more massive than Earth, it has a far greater gravitational pull. Inversely, the same object weighs less on the Moon. Since the Moon is smaller than Earth, its gravitational pull is smaller as well. As a result, a person could lift huge objects on the Moon that he or she could barely move on Earth.

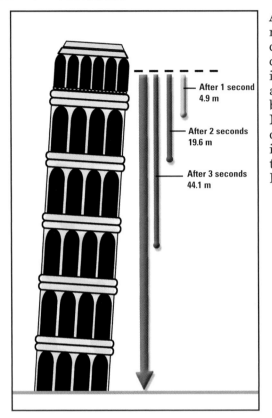

After 1 second
4.9 m

After 2 seconds
19.6 m

After 3 seconds
44.1 m

A dropped object picks up more and more speed and covers a greater distance the closer it gets to the earth, as illustrated at left. This acceleration due to gravity is affected by geography. For instance, New York City's acceleration due to gravity is greater than in a place with higher elevation, such as Denver or Pikes Peak, Colorado.

Physicists speak of the strength of a gravitational field in terms of g, which represents the rate of acceleration of a falling object because of gravity. On Earth, g is 9.8 meters per second per second. This means that two seconds after an object is dropped, it will be moving 9.8 meters per second faster than it did at the end of the first second.

At different places on Earth, g is often slightly less or slightly more than 9.8 meters per second per second. The differences are due to variations in the density of Earth's crust. In fact, geologists use the measurement of g to learn about the movements of the crust. The acceleration due to gravity also differs on various bodies based on the strength of their gravitational field. On the Moon, for instance, g is only about 1.6 meters per second per second, while on Jupiter it is about 24.9 meters per second per second.

	DATE	HIGH				LOW				☼	
		AM	hgt	PM	hgt	AM	hgt	PM	hgt	rise	set
1	Sun	11:54	10.9	-	-	5:54	-1.3	6:07	-0.3	5:20	7:57
2	Mon	12:09	12.3	12:45	11.0	6:45	-1.3	7:01	-0.3	5:21	7:55
3	Tue	1:01	12.1	1:36	11.1	7:35	-1.1	7:54	-0.2	5:22	7:54
4	Wed	1:53	11.7	2:26	11.0	8:25	-0.7	8:47	0.0	5:23	7:53
5	Thu	2:45	11.1	3:15	10.7	9:13	-0.2	9:40	0.3	5:24	7:52
6	Fri	3:38	10.4	4:06	10.5	10:03	0.4	10:35	0.7	5:25	7:50
7	Sat	4:32	9.8	4:57	10.2	10:54	1.0	11:31	1.0	5:27	7:49
8	Sun	5:29	9.2	5:50	9.9	11:47	1.5	-	-	5:28	7:47
9	Mon	6:27	8.8	6:46	9.7	12:29	1.2	12:42	1.9	5:29	7:46
10	Tue	7:27	8.6	7:41	9.7	1:28	1.3	1:38	2.1	5:30	7:44
11	Wed	8:24	8.6	8:35	9.8	2:24	1.3	2:34	2.1	5:31	7:43
12	Thu	9:16	8.7	9:24	10.0	3:17	1.1	3:25	1.9	5:32	7:41
13	Fri	10:03	9.0	10:09	10.2	4:04	0.8	4:11	1.7	5:34	7:40
14	Sat	10:44	9.2	10:51	10.5	4:47	0.6	4:53	1.4	5:35	7:38
15	Sun	11:23	9.5	11:29	10.7	5:26	0.4	5:32	1.2	5:36	7:37
16	Mon	11:58	9.8	-	-	6:02	0.2	6:10	1.0	5:37	7:35
17	Tue	12:05	10.8	12:33	10.0	6:37	0.1	6:46	0.8	5:38	7:34
18	Wed	12:42	10.8	1:07	10.3	7:11	0.0	7:24	0.6	5:39	7:32
19	Thu	1:20	10.8	1:44	10.5	7:46	0.0	8:04	0.4	5:40	7:30
20	Fri	2:00	10.7	2:23	10.7	8:24	0.1	8:47	0.3	5:42	7:29
21	Sat	2:44	10.4	3:07	10.8	9:05	0.3	9:36	0.3	5:43	7:27
22	Sun	3:33	10.1	3:56	10.9	9:52	0.6	10:30	0.3	5:44	7:25
23	Mon	4:28	9.8	4:51	10.8	10:45	0.9	11:31	0.4	5:45	7:24
24	Tue	5:30	9.5	5:52	10.8	11:45	1.1	-	-	5:46	7:22
25	Wed	6:38	9.3	6:59	10.9	12:37	0.3	12:51	1.2	5:47	7:20
26	Thu	7:47	9.5	8:06	11.2	1:46	0.2	2:00	1.1	5:49	7:19
27	Fri	8:53	9.8	9:11	11.5	2:51	-0.2	3:06	0.7	5:50	7:17
28	Sat	9:52	10.3	10:09	11.8	3:52	-0.5	4:07	0.2	5:51	7:15

WINTER HARBOR — Frenchman Bay 44°23'N 068°05'W

August Tide Chart 2004

This is the August 2004 tide chart for Winter Harbor, Maine. Tides are created because of the Sun and Moon's gravity and their cycles of rotation. Because of the predictability of these cycles, scientists can guess the time of high and low tides each day. Each rotation cycle—twenty-four hours and fifty-two minutes—causes two high tides and two low tides.

Practical Applications

On Earth, the gravitational pull of the other bodies in our solar system is most obvious in the behavior of the ocean. The phenomenon of tides results from force exerted by the Moon and, to some extent, the Sun. In general, the water of the oceans on the side of Earth closest to the Moon is pulled up by the Moon's gravitational pull, creating a high tide. Our knowledge of gravitation, therefore, allows us to predict the tidal flow.

Our exploration of space also relies on our understanding of the gravitational force. In order to escape Earth's atmosphere, objects sent into space have to be traveling fast enough to escape its gravitational pull. The laws of gravitation allow us to calculate the necessary speed, known as escape velocity.

They also make it possible to place satellites in orbit. Although Earth is constantly pulled toward the Sun, it does not collide into it because Earth moves at its own velocity. Similarly, a satellite must have the proper velocity to place it in orbit. If its velocity is too small, it will plunge back to Earth. If its velocity is too large, it will overcome the force of gravitation and float away into space.

The Electromagnetic Force

In nearly every moment of our everyday lives, we encounter some phenomenon that is a result of the electromagnetic force. This force is what makes all solid objects solid. It also accounts for light, allowing us to see the world around us. Even the electrical impulses that transmit messages from nerve cells to the brain are governed by the electromagnetic force.

Early Experiments

Since early in human history, people have been fascinated by the effects of both electricity and magnetism. The ancient Greeks and Romans observed how rubbing certain objects against other objects could create an attractive force—what we now call static electricity. For instance, the Greek philosopher Thales in the sixth century BC noticed that after he rubbed a wool cloth against a piece of amber, the amber was able to attract light objects, such as dust and feathers. Thales incorrectly concluded that the force was intrinsic to the amber. But he did help give electricity its name, since the Greek word for amber is "elektron."

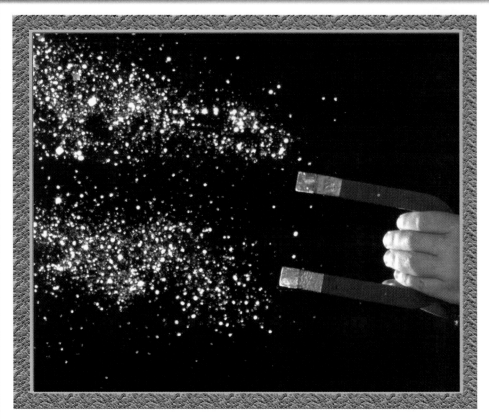

This photograph shows a magnet attracting iron particles. A magnet is simply anything that attracts iron and produces a magnetic field. All elements in the periodic table have some magnetic property.

The ancients also noted that loadstone, now called magnetite, had the power to attract bits of iron placed near it. (The word "magnet" is derived from the fact that loadstone was plentiful in the Magnesia district of Asia Minor.) Humans soon also discovered a more useful property of loadstone: If the stone was suspended from a rope or floated on a piece of wood in a pool of water, the stone would orient itself so that one end pointed north. Probably originating in

China, very simple compasses based on this principle helped ancient travelers find their way.

Exploring Magnetism

At least by the twelfth century AD, sailors used sophisticated compasses to navigate the oceans. But until 1600, no one understood why magnetized compass needles pointed north. In that year, Queen Elizabeth's physician, Sir William Gilbert, wrote a treatise on magnets that consolidated current knowledge about magnetism and created new hypotheses on a magnet's properties.

By Gilbert's day, it was known that a magnet's attractive powers are concentrated at its two ends, called poles. One pole is naturally attracted to the north and one to the south. Unlike poles (north and south) of two magnets attract each other, while like poles (north and north, or south and south) repel each other. On a single magnet, the closer the poles are to each other, the stronger the pull of the magnetic poles will be. (For instance, the pull of the poles of a horseshoe-shaped magnet is naturally stronger than the pull of a bar-shaped magnet's poles.) Furthermore, when a magnet is cut in two, each part becomes a complete magnet, with one north pole and one south pole.

Previously, the only known magnets were made from loadstone. Gilbert, however, discovered that by rubbing a natural loadstone magnet against an iron bar, he could turn the iron into an artificial magnet. Another important part of Gilbert's treatise was a new theory about why north poles point north and south poles point south. Gilbert hypothesized that Earth itself is an enormous magnet, with its own north pole and south pole. As it was later discovered, these magnetic poles do not confirm exactly with the geographic poles of Earth. Thus, navigators using magnetic compasses had to make calculations to off-set this distance and keep their ships on course.

Studying Electricity

By the early eighteenth century, scientists were also developing new theories about electricity. Based on observing simple experiments with static electricity, scientists came to believe there were two separate electrical forces—one that attracted and one that repelled. Working in England, Stephen Gray found that electrical forces travel through some substances more easily than others. And in the United States, Benjamin Franklin's famous kite experiment established that lightning was a natural form of electricity.

A major breakthrough in our understanding of the electric force occurred in 1820. A paper published by Danish physicist Hans Christian Oersted recounted an interesting discovery. He found that if an electric current passed through a wire and that

An electromagnet is a magnetic field created by an electric current. When a wire is connected to the positive and negative ends of a battery and placed near a compass, the compass needle will move from its natural resting place (north). Electrons flow from the negative end of the battery through the wire to the positive end, generating a small magnetic field in the wire.

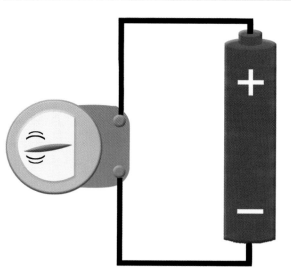

wire was placed near a compass, the compass's needle moved. Oersted concluded that an electrical current could create a magnetic force.

Oersted's discovery led to one of the most important tools of industry—the electromagnet. This type of artificial magnet is created by winding a coil of wire around an iron bar. When a current is sent through the wire, the iron is magnetized. When the current is turned off, the bar loses nearly all of its magnetic force.

But Oersted's work was just as significant for its suggestion that electricity and magnetism were more closely related than previously thought. His work inspired more experiments involving these two forces.

One Force

This study reached a turning point with the work of English physicist Michael Faraday in the 1830s.

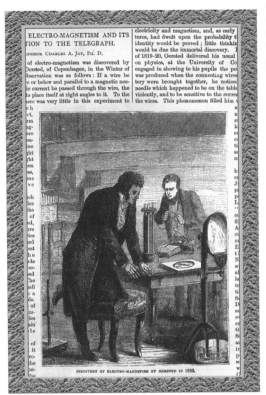

ELECTRO-MAGNETISM AND ITS TION TO THE TELEGRAPH.

Hans Christian Oersted's discovery that electricity could create magnetism led to important developments regarding the electromagnetic force. This illustration shows Oersted working in his lab with a colleague. It was published alongside an article entitled "History of Electro-magnetism and Its Application to the Telegraph," in *Frank Leslie's Popular Monthly*.

From Oersted's work, Faraday knew electricity could produce a magnetic effect. Faraday wondered whether the inverse were true—if magnetism could produce an electrical effect. His experiments suggested that electricity and magnetism were in fact different manifestations of one force. Faraday also theorized that electricity and magnetism exerted themselves in invisible "lines of force," suggesting the concept of an electromagnetic field—an area where the magnetic and electrical effects of a moving electric charge are felt.

By the mid-nineteenth century, the experiments of Oersted, Faraday, and others suggested a number of new ideas about electricity and magnetism. In the 1860s and 1870s, these were brought together into a coherent theory by the Scottish physicist James Clerk Maxwell. He devised a set of equations that mathematically confirmed that electricity and magnetism were a single unified force.

Maxwell also theorized that a magnetic field produced by an oscillating electrical charge expands outward at a constant speed. He calculated this speed to be about 300,000 kilometers per second, close to the speed of light. From this, Maxwell hypothesized that light was a form of electromagnetic radiation that travels in waves. His idea also suggested that there were other forms of electromagnetic energy invisible to the eye, thereby predicting the existence of radio waves and X-rays.

Electromagnetism and the Atom

Arguably, Maxwell's theories were as important to understanding the electromagnetic force as Newton's were to understanding the gravitational force. However, in several ways, the two theories contradicted each other. Inspired to resolve these contradictions, Albert Einstein developed his theories of special and general relativity. While Einstein's work upended Newton's view of the gravitational force, it generally confirmed Maxwell's theories.

During the early twentieth century, advances in particle physics also helped solve remaining mysteries about the electromagnetic force. From Maxwell's time, physicists knew much about how the electromagnetic force functions, but little about why. The answers came with the study of the subatomic particles that make up all matter.

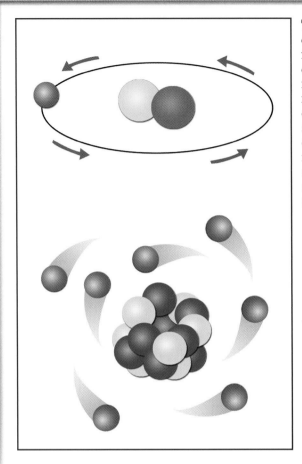

The motion of an electrical charge produces a magnetic field. In the top example, an electron orbits the nucleus, made up of a proton and a neutron. As the electron orbits the nucleus, it also spins, just as Earth rotates during its orbit. Niels Bohr's model of the atom *(below)* shows that electrons don't orbit in the same patterns on every revolution.

Early models of the atom identified three elementary particles—the electron, the proton, and the neutron. The proton and the neutron were housed in the atom's nucleus, and the electrons orbited around it.

Physicists found that atoms are held together by the electrical charges of these particles. Electrons have a negative charge, and protons have a positive charge. (Neutrons, as the name implies, are neutral, having no charge at all.) The unlike charges of the electrons and protons create the electromagnetic force that glues these subatomic particles to one another.

Orbiting electrons, however, are not firmly attached to the nucleus. They might break free from their atom and join another. Electrical charge results from this exchange of electrons. An atom with a deficit of electrons becomes positively charged, while one with an excess of electrons becomes negatively charged.

An electric current is produced when circumstances allow for the free flow of electrons in and out of atoms. In some substances, such as copper and silver, electrons can move easily. They are called conductors. In others, like rubber and glass, electrons can barely move at all. These are known as insulators.

The phenomenon of magnetism can also be understood in terms of electrons. As they orbit the nucleus, the electrons spin, creating a weak magnetic field. In most substances, half the electrons spin in one direction, while the second half spin in the other—a condition that essentially cancels out the magnetic effect. But in a few substances, including iron and nickel, the spin of the electrons is not divided equally in the two directions, which makes them easy to magnetize. These substances are called ferromagnetic.

As the power behind phenomena large and small, the electromagnetic force affects us in a multitude of ways. Its influence extends throughout nature—making the sky glow with lightning, dictating the chemical reactions in our bodies, allowing for the existence of visible light, and, perhaps most important of all, forming the atoms that make up everything around us.

Electromagnetism at Work

The importance of the electromagnetic force extends beyond its responsibility for natural phenomena. It also makes possible the many machines and devices that we rely on daily. This force powers everything from factory machinery to electric lights to household appliances. In fact, our ability to harness the power of the electromagnetic force is one of the defining characteristics of the contemporary world.

Magnets Around Us

Most of the magnets we notice in our day-to-day lives perform fairly unexciting tasks—perhaps holding a note to a refrigerator or keeping a cabinet door shut. But, hidden from view, magnets are at work in many of the industrial machines and household appliances we routinely use.

Permanent magnets do not require an electrical field and remain magnetized for a long time. They are used in many types of machinery—from traffic lights to the seismographs that measure the intensity of an earthquake to the cardiographs that record

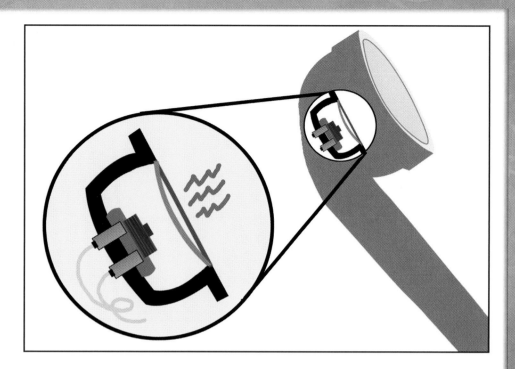

This diagram shows a detail of a telephone receiver, which holds an electromagnet in its earpiece (shown in red). An electrical current sent from the telephone network flows through the electromagnet and creates a magnetic field. A flexible iron disk (in blue) in the earpiece becomes attracted to the magnetic field and moves in and out depending on the electrical current. This movement creates air, which creates sound.

human heartbeats. They are also found in lathes, conveyors, and hand tools.

Electromagnets are even more prevalent. For instance, every telephone receiver contains an electromagnet to record the vibrations of the speaker's voice. Nearly everything powered by an electric motor also makes use of an electromagnet. Small electromagnets are found in most factory machinery. Giant electromagnets are used in steel plants and on railroad yards to move heavy loads of steel and iron. In the home, electromagnets make possible a

Magnetic Bottles

Magnets play an important role in producing energy in nuclear fusion reactors. Within a reactor, plasma is heated to as high as 100 million degrees Celsius. Storing the heated plasma is difficult. At such high temperatures, matter can exist only as charged particles in the center, which would vaporize instantly if they touched the side of a conventional container. Instead, they are stored in magnetic bottles, in which a magnetic field holds the particles, keeping them away from the container's walls.

wide array of appliances—blenders, washing machines, drills, and shavers, just to name a few.

Motors and Generators

In fact, nearly any machine powered by an electric motor contains a magnet. Motors operate under the principle of electromagnetic induction. This principle holds that if an electric current flows through a wire and the wire is placed in a magnetic field, the electromagnetic force will cause the wire to move.

When a motor is turned on, current travels along a coil of wire on an axle surrounded by a magnet. Its magnetic field causes the wire and axle to rotate. In this way, the electromagnetic force allows a motor to convert electrical energy into mechanical energy.

Generators also make use of electromagnetic induction, but for the opposite effect. These devices convert mechanical energy into electrical energy. In a simple generator, a conductor, often a coil of wire, is rotated between a magnet's poles. The coil passes through the magnetic field, first in one direction, then in the other. As a result, an alternating electrical current—moving in one direction, then the next—flows through the conductor. The current's strength depends on the strength of the field, the length of the conductor, and the speed at which the conductor moves through the field. Large generators may have several coils and magnets to increase their energy output.

In practical terms, the invention of the generator was perhaps the most significant consequence of the discovery of electromagnetism. Because of generators, we can easily make use of electricity, an extremely convenient form of energy. Our ability to generate, store, and transmit electricity allows us to operate industrial machinery, light our homes and streets, and operate appliances, computers, televisions, and a host of other electrical devices. In this way, without our current understanding of the electromagnetic force, modern life as we know it would be impossible.

Making Waves

In the nineteenth century, our knowledge of the electromagnetic force ushered in the industrial age. In the twentieth century, it spurred another era—the information age. Physicists' understanding of electromagnetic waves paved the way for many revolutionary inventions.

Electromagnetic waves all travel through space at roughly the speed of light. They differ from each other, however, in the frequency at which their electrical and magnetic fields oscillate. This accounts for the different waves on the electromagnetic spectrum, including microwaves, radio and television waves, ultraviolet waves, gamma rays, and X-rays.

More recently, scientists have learned how to concentrate electromagnetic waves into laser beams. Lasers are increasingly used in place of knives for surgical procedures. They also make it possible to record electronic data on CDs and DVDs.

Other Applications

The laws that govern the electromagnetic force have many other practical applications. For instance, the principle that like magnetic poles repulse each other is used in sophisticated rail systems. Through magnetic repulsion, trains are slightly suspended above the tracks, which eliminates friction between the trains and the metal rails.

Another application of electromagnetic theory includes electrolysis and electroplating. Electrolysis is the process of using an electrical current to bring about a chemical reaction. It is particularly useful for purifying copper and extracting aluminum. Through electroplating, a cheap metal, such as steel, can be coated with a thin layer of a more costly

Electromagnets are being used in the development of high-speed maglev (short for "magnetic levitation") trains. Instead of the traditional wheels-on-a-track construction, the maglev train uses magnetic propulsion, so that the train floats over its path. The magnetized coils on the sides repel magnets that are attached to the bottom of the train, allowing the train to hover about 3 inches (7.6 cm) above the guideway. An electric current of varying strength is supplied to metal coils on the guideway, creating a magnetic field that propels the train forward.

metal to improve its appearance or durability. Steel car bumpers, for instance, are often coated with chromium to protect them from corrosion.

By the laws of electromagnetism, when charged particles move through a magnetic field, the course of their movement is deflected. Television picture tubes and oscilloscopes use this principle to deflect beams of particles. Even more important to physicists, this principle allows them to control the path of a particle traveling in a particle accelerator, a device essential in studying the fundamental particles that make up all matter. In an accelerator, a physicist can deflect

This computer visualization shows the tunnel of the Large Hadron Collider, a particle accelerator near Geneva, Switzerland. Physicists use particle accelerators to study interactions of the particles (most often protons and electrons) that make up matter.

particles and increase their momentum. Traveling at high speeds, the particles are then smashed into their component parts. Through accelerator experiments, physicists in the last fifty years have made enormous strides in understanding our universe. Central to that understanding was the discovery of two previously unimagined fundamental forces that control the behavior of elementary particles.

The Strong and Weak Forces

For more than 100 years, physicists have had a solid understanding of the gravitational force and the electromagnetic force. But just in recent decades they have confirmed earlier theories about the two other fundamental forces—the weak force and the strong force. An understanding of these two forces emerged only after the birth of quantum mechanics. This branch of physics deals with behavior of the elementary particles that make up all matter.

Finding the Strong Force

The scientific study of atoms as fundamental particles began in the nineteenth century. But by the 1920s, physicists determined that atoms were themselves made up of smaller particles. In early models of the atom, these particles were identified as the proton (positively charged), electron (negatively charged), and neutron (neutral charge).

This model, however, created a problem for physicists. By the laws of electromagnetism, the positively

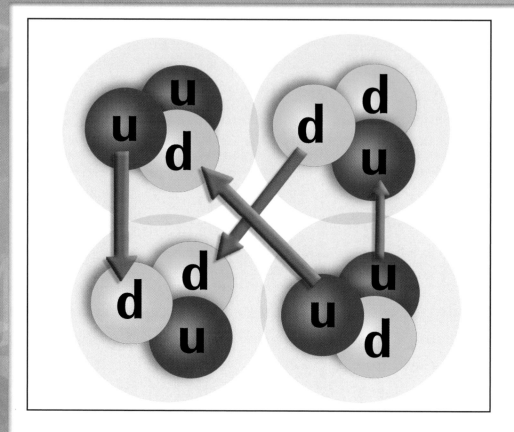

The above diagram illustrates the strong force. Protons and neutrons are made up of quarks (the up and the down are labeled), which are attracted by the strong force, carried by gluons. This force binds quarks together and overcomes the natural repulsion that occurs in an atom.

charged protons in the nucleus should repel one another. At the same time, of course, protons are attracted to one another because of the gravitational force. But gravitation is a much weaker force than the electromagnetic force. If these were the only forces at work in the atom, no nucleus could hold together for long.

The puzzle was solved as physicists' model of the atom became more sophisticated. They now know that protons and neutrons are made up of still smaller particles called quarks. Both protons and neutrons are made up of three quarks each.

Still another particle accounts for the force that attracts the quarks in one proton to the quarks in another. These particles are called gluons. In the exchange of gluons, an attractive force binds the quarks of protons, overcoming the repulsive force of their like electrical charges.

This force that holds the nucleus together is now known as the strong force. It acts across only a very short range. But, as its name implies, it is relatively strong.

Discovering the Weak Force

Like the strong force, the weak force is exerted only on the subatomic level. And like the strong force, its existence was theorized by physicists long before it could be proven.

In the early years of the twentieth century, the experiments of English physicist Ernest Rutherford indicated that there are three types of radiation— alpha, beta, and gamma. As physicists further studied these phenomena, they found that alpha and gamma radiation could be explained by the laws known to govern the gravitational force and the strong force.

But beta decay proved more of a mystery. A radioactive element experiences beta decay when the

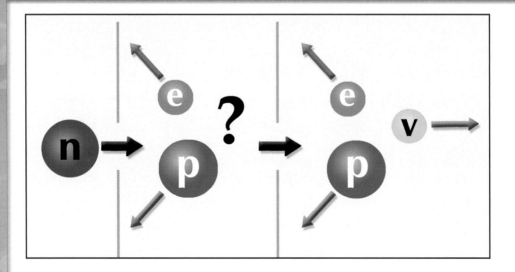

This illustration shows the beta decay process. A neutron (n) decays into a proton (p) and an electron (e). A neutrino (v) is emitted in the process to maintain momentum and balance of energy.

nuclei of its atoms are unstable because of an excess of neutrons. As it decays, a neutron spits out a negatively charged electron and, in the process, turns into a positively charged proton. The trouble for physicists, however, is that a certain amount of energy released by the exchange was unaccounted for.

German physicist Wolfgang Pauli first theorized that another, formerly unknown particle was released during beta decay, which would account for the excess energy. Drawing on Pauli's work, Enrico Fermi of Italy dubbed this new particle a neutrino, since it had a neutral charge. He also postulated that there was a fourth force in nature that regulated the transformation of a neutron into an electron, a proton, and a neutrino. In 1959, experiments confirmed

The First Matter

The weak force may have been responsible for the creation of the stars, planets, and everything else in the universe. Some physicists believe that, when the universe was young, most matter was made of neutrinos. If so, these particles were generated through radioactive decay governed by the weak force.

the neutrino's existence, validating Fermi's ideas. The fourth force became known as the weak force.

The W and Z Particles

More recent study of the weak force has revealed that still another particle is involved in beta decay. In the 1970s, physicists theorized that, like the strong force, the weak force requires a force carrier. In 1983, using the CERN particle accelerator in Switzerland, several researchers observed this particle, named the W particle after the weak force. Three months later, the CERN physicists found a second particle, the Z particle, that is also involved in weak interactions. For their discoveries, they were awarded the Nobel Prize in Physics the following year.

W and Z particles are relatively large. But the life of W and Z particles is short. They exist for only a fraction of a second needed to fulfill their role in the decay of a particle during a weak interaction.

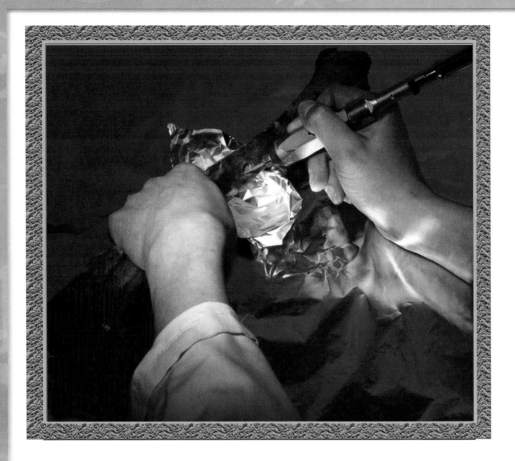

In this photograph, a scientist takes a sample of a reindeer's bone for radiocarbon dating. Radiocarbon dating is an example of the effect of the weak force and has helped scientists in many fields understand the past.

In beta decay, for example, a neutron (0 charge) first changes into a proton (+1 charge) and a W particle (-1 charge). Almost immediately, the W particle transforms into an electron (-1 charge) and a neutrino (0 charge). The net charge from the decay of the neutron is zero, thereby obeying the fundamental law of physics that calls for the conservation of charge.

The Weak Force in the World

Weak interactions are relatively rare on Earth, but they do play a role in some familiar phenomena. One instance is radioactive dating, which is used to date ancient objects. Most radioactive dating involves carbon 14, which, through beta decay, turns into nitrogen over time. By measuring the amount of carbon 14 and nitrogen in an object, scientists can determine the object's age. The weak interaction is also responsible for the decay of radon. Decaying radon found in homes has been linked to lung cancer.

But aside from beta decay, the weak force has its greatest effect on our world because it governs hydrogen fusion. In this process, four hydrogen nuclei combine to form neutrinos and a helium nucleus. Hydrogen fusion creates the Sun's energy. Since the Sun's heat and energy make life on Earth possible, we in a sense owe our very existence to the weak force.

The Unification of Forces

About thirteen billion years ago, the universe came into being with the big bang. Physicists believe that in the earliest moments after this explosion, the four fundamental forces were actually one. Only as the universe cooled did the gravitational, electromagnetic, strong, and weak forces emerge.

Physicists have long tried to turn back the clock, hoping to discover the underlying unity of the various forces of nature. The discovery that electricity and magnetism were the same force was an early step toward unification. In the twentieth century, Albert Einstein attempted to take the next one as he tried to reconcile the laws of gravitation based on his general theory of relativity with Maxwell's laws of electromagnetism. Despite thirty years of effort, Einstein failed to develop a complete unified field theory.

The Electroweak Theory

In more recent years, however, physicists focusing on unification have made significant progress, making the search for reconciling the four forces one of the most dynamic fields of modern physics.

The greatest success in this field of study was the development of the electroweak theory. In the 1960s, working independently, three physicists—Sheldon Glashow, Abdus Salam, and Steven Weinberg—tried to reconcile oddities in our understanding of the weak force by applying principles derived by the theory of electromagnetic force. They all were able to show mathematically that the electromagnetic force and the weak force are different manifestations of the same force. In 1978, this idea was confirmed experimentally. Glashow, Salam, and Weinberg won the Nobel Prize for their pioneering work.

Sheldon Glashow, Abdus Salam, and Steven Weinberg *(left to right)* wait to receive their Nobel Prize for Physics in 1979. The three scientists were awarded the great honor for their work on the electroweak theory.

The electroweak theory helped physicists build the standard model for particle physics. The standard model is a theory that describes all known particles and three forces (electromagnetic, weak, and strong) that act upon them. It established three families of elementary particles—quarks, leptons, and bosons. Bosons are force carriers. The known bosons are

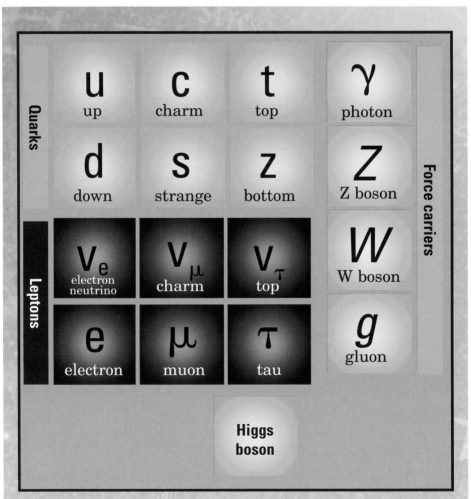

The theory of the standard model encompasses the strong force, the weak force, and the electromagnetic force. Although the standard model has been regarded as a success, it still has not been accepted as a complete theory.

the photon (electromagnetic force carrier), gluon (strong force carrier), and W and Z particles (weak force carriers). Physicists postulate the existence of a fourth particle—the graviton—that carries the gravitational force, but it has never been observed.

The electroweak theory, though, also posed plenty of new questions about how two seemingly unrelated phenomena could be unified. For instance, the electromagnetic force works over an infinite range. The weak force, on the other hand, works only over distances smaller than the nucleus of an atom. The disparity in the mass of the two forces' carriers was also peculiar. The photon is massless, while the W and Z particles are among the largest elementary particles.

The Higgs Boson

The difference in the mass of known force carriers was part of a larger question that troubled physicists: Why do particles have any mass at all? One possible answer came from Scottish physicist Peter Higgs in the mid-1960s. Higgs's theory suggested that there is a lattice-like field that fills the universe. As a particle passes through this field, it creates a distortion that gives the particle its mass. The mass of a particle would then depend on how strongly it interacts with this field.

In Higgs's theory, this interaction would be governed by a new type of force-carrying particle, now called the Higgs boson. Since this hypothetical boson would be responsible for all matter in the universe, it has earned the nickname the God particle.

Using particle accelerators, researchers are coming ever closer to proving the existence or nonexistence of the Higgs boson. If the boson is found, the discovery will lead to an overhaul of our standard model governing particles and the forces that act on them.

Toward a Unified Theory

Physicists are also close to developing what is called the grand unified theory. This theory would unify not only the electromagnetic force and the weak force, but the strong force as well. The mathematical theories about all three forces show similarities that suggest such a theory might be possible.

Building a theory that unites all four forces presents more of a challenge, since the mathematical structure of gravitation is quite different. Einstein's general theory of relativity remains our best theory for understanding the gravitational force.

But physicists working toward a complete unification theory have some intriguing leads. Of the most promising are five different string theories. All of these theories hold that particles should be seen not as pointlike objects, but as vibrating strings. The theories also postulate that the four forces exist in ten dimensions. String theories are attractive to physicists because their mathematical underpinnings seem able to account for gravity. Very recently, evidence suggests that the five string theories are actually versions of one fundamental theory, now referred to as M-theory.

No one knows when we will be able to unify the four fundamental forces in nature. A young physics student might discover the answer tomorrow. Or it might take teams of theoretical physicists another fifty years, or even a hundred years, to solve the puzzle. But we do know one thing: When a unification theory emerges, it will help reshape our understanding of our universe and of ourselves.

Glossary

electromagnetic force (ih-LEK-troh-mag-NET-ik FORS) A fundamental force involving the electric and magnetic effects of particles.

electron (ih-LEK-tron) A negatively charged particle that orbits an atom's nucleus.

electroweak theory (ih-LEK-tro-week THEE-ih-ree) A theory that unifies the electromagnetic force and the weak force.

ferromagnetic (fair-oh-mag-NET-ik) Relating to substances, such as iron and nickel, that can be easily magnetized.

gravitational force (grav-i-TAY-shun-al FORS) The attractive force that exists between two objects or particles.

insulator (IN-soo-lay-ter) A substance that resists the flow of an electric current.

mass (MAS) The amount of matter in an object.

matter (MAH-ter) Something that occupies space, has mass, and exists as a solid, liquid, or gas.

neutron (NOO-tron) A neutral particle within an atom's nucleus.

proton (PRO-ton) A positively charged particle within an atom's nucleus.

quark (KWARK) An elementary particle that makes up neutrons and protons.

radiation (ray-dee-AY-shun) Energy transmitted as waves, rays, or particles.

strong force (STRONG FORS) The fundamental force that binds neutrons and protons within an atom's nucleus.

weak force (WEEK FORS) The fundamental force that dictates beta decay and hydrogen fusion.

weight (WAYT) The force that attracts an object to Earth.

For More Information

American Center for Physics
One Physics Ellipse
College Park, MD 20740
(301) 209-3100
Web site: http://www.acp.org

National Aeronautic Space Administration
300 E Street SW
Washington, DC 20546
(202) 358-0000
Web site: http://nasa.gov/home/index.html

National Air and Science Museum
Smithsonian Institution
Washington, DC 20560
(202) 357-2700
Web site: http://www.nasm.si.edu/museum/flagship.cfm

National Science Foundation (Math and Physical Sciences)
4201 Wilson Boulevard
Arlington, VA 22230
(703) 292-5111
Web site: http://www.nsf.gov/home/mps

Web Sites

Due to the changing nature of Internet links, the Rosen Publishing Group, Inc., has developed an online list of Web sites related to the subject of this book. This site is updated regularly. Please use this link to access the list:

http://www.rosenlinks.com/liph/fona

For Further Reading

Close, Frank, Michael Marten, and Christine Sutton. *The Particle Odyssey: A Journey to the Heart of Matter.* New York: Oxford University Press, 2002.

Green, Brian. *Elegant Universe: Superstrings, Hidden Dimensions, and the Quest for the Ultimate Theory.* New York: Vintage, 2000.

Math, Irwin. *Wires and Watts: Understanding and Using Electricity.* New York: Aladdin Books, 1989.

McGrath, Kimberley A. *World of Physics.* Detroit: Gale, 2001.

Russell, Colin Archibald. *Michael Faraday: Physics and Faith.* New York: Oxford University Press, 2001.

Volti, Rudi. *The Facts on File Encyclopedia of Science, Technology, and Society.* New York: Facts on File, 1999.

Bibliography

Close, Frank, Michael Marten, and Christine Sutton. *The Particle Odyssey: A Journey to the Heart of Matter.* New York: Oxford University Press, 2002.

"The Great Unifier." *Discover.* May 2002,. Vol. 23, p. 18.

"Ideas." Exploratorium. Retrieved March 2004 (http://www.exploratorium.edu/origins/cern/ideas).

McGrath, Kimberley A. *World of Physics.* Detroit: Gale, 2001.

New Book of Popular Science. Danbury, CT: Grolier Educational, 2004.

"The Particle Adventure." Lawrence Berkeley National Laboratory. Retrieved March 2004 (http://www.particleadventure.org/particleadventure).

Rincon, Paul. "'God Particle' May Have Been Seen." BBC News Online. March 10, 2004. Retrieved March 2004 (http://news.bbc.co.uk/2/hi/science/nature/3546973.stm).

Seife, Charles. "Shadowy 'Weak Force' Steps into the Light." *Science*. July 12, 2002, Vol. 297. p. 184.

Spotts, Peter N. "A Massive Mystery." *Christian Science Monitor.* October 5, 2000, Vol. 92, p. 13.

U*X*L Encyclopedia of Science. 2nd ed. Detroit: Gale, 2004.

Virtual Visitor Center. Stanford Linear Accelerator Center. Retrieved May 2004 (http://www2.slac.stanford.edu/vvc).

Volti, Rudi. *The Facts on File Encyclopedia of Science, Technology, and Society.* New York: Facts on File, 1999.

Weinberg, Steven. "A Unified Physics by 2050?" *Scientific American.* March 1, 2003, p. 8.

Index

About the Author

Liz Sonneborn is a writer and an editor, living in Brooklyn, New York. A graduate of Swarthmore College, she has written more than thirty books for children and adults, including *The American West*, *A to Z of American Women in the Performing Arts*, and *The New York Public Library's Amazing Native American History*, winner of a 2000 Parent's Choice Award.

Photo Credits

Cover © NASA/Science Source/ Photo Researchers, Inc.; pp. 7, 40 © Bettmann/Corbis; pp. 9, 12, 19, 22, 25, 29, 32, 34 by Geraldine Fletcher; p. 10 © Yannick Mellier/IAP/Photo Researchers; p. 13 courtesy of MaineHarbors.com; p. 16 © Custom Stock Medical Photo; p. 20 © Corbis; p. 30 © CERN/Photo Researchers, Inc.; p. 36 © James King-Holmes/Science Photo Library; p. 39 by Tahara Anderson.

Designer: Tahara Anderson; Editor: Christine Poolos